The Billy Goats Gruff

A play by Julia Donaldson

Illustrated by Steve Horrocks

Characters

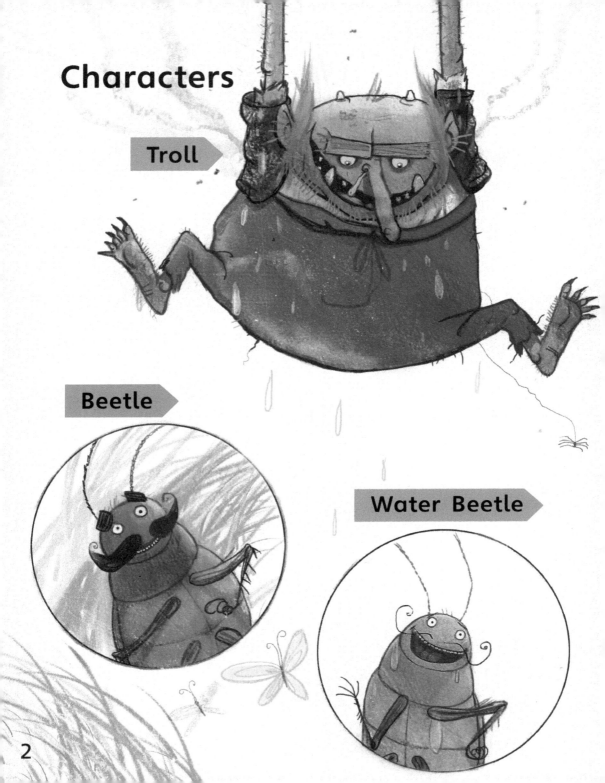

Troll

Beetle

Water Beetle

Little
(Little Billy Goat Gruff)

Big
(Big Billy
Goat Gruff)

Middle
(Middle Billy Goat Gruff)

3

Beetle: Hello! I'm a beetle. Who are you?

Water Beetle: I'm a beetle too – a water beetle. I live in this river.

Beetle: That's a funny place to live!

Water Beetle: No it's not. Lots of creatures live in the river. Fish, tadpoles, newts …

Troll: AND ME!

Beetle: Who are you?

Troll: I'M A TROLL.

Beetle: Help! I hope you don't like eating beetles!

Troll: NO, I LIKE EATING GOATS!

Beetle: Phew!

Water Beetle: Where do you live, Beetle?

Beetle: I live in this field.

Water Beetle: That's a funny place to live!

Beetle: No it's not. Lots of creatures live here. Worms, moles, rabbits ...

Little: And us!

Water Beetle: Who are you?

Middle: We're the three Billy Goats Gruff.

Big: I'm Big Billy Goat Gruff.

Middle: I'm Middle Billy Goat Gruff.

Little: And I'm Little Billy Goat Gruff.

Beetle: I hope you don't like eating beetles!

Big: No, we like eating grass.

Little: But the grass in this field is all brown.

Water Beetle: The grass on the other side of the river is better.

Little: Excellent! Let's go and try that.

Big: But that means crossing the bridge.

Middle: So what?

Big: There's a troll under the bridge.

Water Beetle: Yes, and he loves eating goats.

9

Little: Eek!

Middle: What can we do?

Big: I have a plan.

Big whispers to the other goats.

Beetle: Look, Little Billy Goat Gruff is crossing the bridge.

Water Beetle: Trip trap, trip trap! The troll will hear him!

Troll: Who's that trip-trapping over my bridge?

Little: It's me, Little Billy Goat Gruff.

Troll: You look good. I'm going to eat you!

Little:	Oh no, don't eat **me**! Wait for Middle Billy Goat Gruff.
Troll:	Why?
Little:	He's bigger than me.
Troll:	All right. I'll wait for him.
Beetle:	Look, Little Billy Goat Gruff has crossed the bridge.

Big: Your turn, Middle Billy Goat Gruff.

Water Beetle: Trip trap, trip trap! The troll will hear him!

Troll: Who's that trip-trapping over my bridge?

Middle: It's me, Middle Billy Goat Gruff.

Troll: You look tasty. I'm going to eat you!

weee!

Middle: Don't eat **me**! Wait for Big Billy Goat Gruff. He's much bigger than me.

Troll: All right then. I'll wait for him.

14

Beetle: Look! Middle Billy Goat Gruff has crossed the bridge.

Little: Hello, Middle Billy Goat Gruff! Have some of this green grass. It's delicious.

Water Beetle: Here comes Big Billy Goat Gruff.

Beetle: Tramp-stamp, tramp-stamp! What a din!

Troll: Who's that tramp-stamping over my bridge?

Big: It's me, Big Billy Goat Gruff.

Troll: You look juicy! I'm going to eat you!

Big: That's what you think!

Troll: Why, what do you think?

Big: I think I'm going to butt you!

Troll: Help!

Beetle: Watch out, Water Beetle! The troll is tumbling into the water.

18

Water Beetle: What a splash! And now Big Billy Goat Gruff is over the bridge.

Little: Hello, Big Billy Goat Gruff! Have some of this delicious green grass.

Middle: Good old Big Billy Goat Gruff! Your plan worked.

Big: That troll won't get us now!

Troll: Grrr!

Beetles: Well done, Billy Goats Gruff!